ATTACKED

LORETTA SCHORR

ASTONISHING HEADLINES

Attacked	Missing
Captured	Shot Down
Condemned	Stowed Away
Kidnapped	Stranded at Sea
Lost and Found	Trapped

Development: Kent Publishing Services, Inc.
Design and Production: Signature Design Group, Inc.

SADDLEBACK EDUCATIONAL PUBLISHING
3120 Pullman Street
Costa Mesa, CA 92626

Website: www.sdlback.com

Photo Credits: cover, Luke Frazza, Agence France Presse;
page 17, Picture History; page 29, PR Newswire Photo
Service; page 38, Ron Kuntz, Reuters Photo Archive

ISBN-13: 978-1-56254-814-8
ISBN-10: 1-56254-814-X
eBook: 978-1-60291-004-1

Printed in the United States of America
13 12 11 10 3 4 5 6 7 8 9

TABLE OF CONTENTS

Introduction

In the busy city of Boston, men argued with the British King who was far away in Britain. They wanted to be free. But the king's men attacked. After the Boston Massacre of 1770, a new country was born.

On a calm Sunday morning in 1941, ships sat in Pearl Harbor. Men slept. They did not see the planes flying low. After the Japanese attacked Pearl Harbor that day, our nation entered World War II.

At a college in Kent, Ohio, young people walked arm-in-arm and chanted, "No more war!" But the National Guard soldiers shot into the crowd. After the deaths of four students at Kent State University in 1970, new laws were passed.

In a far away land, people fought over religion and land. Soon, bombs fell in the streets. During the siege of Sarajevo in the 1990s, the United States tried to stop people from killing each other.

In the halls of the Pentagon, workers began their workday. They did not see the plane flying low. After the September 11 attack in 2001, our nation learned to deal with terror.

Could these attacks have been stopped?

Sadly, attacks do happen. Bombs fall. Fires rage. Guns fire. Homes are crushed. Cities are ruined. People are killed. No one is ever the same!

The Boston Massacre

DATAFILE

TIMELINE

March 1770

British soldiers kill five people in Boston.

December 1773

Tea is dumped into Boston harbor to protest English taxes.

July 1776

The War of Independence begins.

Where were the 13 Colonies?

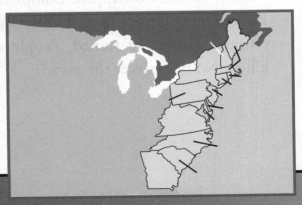

KEY TERMS

protest - to speak out against

colonies - a region politically controlled by a distant country

Britain - also called England and the United Kingdom; a country in Europe

colonists - people who live in colonies

Parliament - the place where laws are made in Britain; the national legislature of Great Britain

represent - to stand in for

DID YOU KNOW?

In the 1700s and 1800s, the colonies of Britain covered nearly one quarter of Earth's surface.

Chapter One:
The Boston Massacre

If you lived in Britain in 1670, would you be brave enough to travel to the British colonies in a new world? This trip would take you 30 days or more!

At that time, the colonies in America were far away and unknown. It was a place to make a new life. Would you be afraid to leave your home and cross the ocean to the British colonies?

Thousands made the trip! Why? Many wanted to buy cheap land, and some wanted to start businesses.

The 13 British Colonies

Connecticut

Delaware

Georgia

Maryland

Massachusetts

New Hampshire

New Jersey

New York

North Carolina

Pennsylvania

Rhode Island

South Carolina

Virginia

Still others wanted to celebrate their own religion. So these brave people took a risk and became colonists. They had many troubles. Life was difficult in the British colonies, but that did not stop them!

By 1750, hundreds of thousands of people left Britain for the British colonies. They were far from home, but the King was still in charge.

Taxes and Laws

The King needed money. Britain had fought a war with France. The King had to pay his soldiers.

To get money, the King created a new tax in March 1765. It was called "The Stamp Act," and it was a tax on legal and other papers. The colonists would start paying the tax in November that same year.

Riots Break Out in Boston

In the British colonies, people did not like paying taxes to the British King. In November 1765, people rioted in Boston. They destroyed a building and a home, and also set fires. Many colonists wanted to protest.

> *"We should have a vote*
> *in Parliament!"*
> *— An unknown colonist*

No one represented the colonists in Parliament. In fact, Parliament passed another law creating more taxes and more rules for the colonists to follow.

The King sent soldiers to the British colonies to make sure the people paid the taxes. The soldiers checked the ships, searched businesses, and even entered people's homes. Would you stand for that? No one wanted soldiers in their homes.

Life in the Colonies

Colonial Times:
1600 - 1780

Clothing

breeches and petticoats

In the Kitchen

pipkins (earthenware pots)

pottage (stew), licorice, raisins

wooden dishes, no utensils

Homes

one or two rooms and no indoor water

Toys & Games

dolls, kites, hide and seek, races

Families

16+ children per family

people begin working at age 6+

Average Lifespan

less than 55 years

Population

1610 - 350 people

1780 - 2,780,400 people

Life in the U.S.A.

Today: 2000s

Clothing
jeans and skirts

In the Kitchen
pans

salad and candy

dishes, spoons, forks, knives

Homes
many rooms, indoor bathrooms and kitchens

Toys & Games
computer games and many more

Families
1-5 children per family

people begin working at age 16+

Average Lifespan
70-85 years

Population
1990 - 248,709,870 people

2000 - 281,421,900 people

The Shooting Starts

The colonists did not like the soldiers. On January 19, 1770, in New York, a mob fought with British soldiers in a field called Golden Hill. Two colonists were shot and many were hurt. But no one was killed.

In Boston, the soldiers and the people often fought. But no one was seriously hurt until March 5, 1770, the day of the Boston Massacre. Although a foot of snow had fallen, many people were out in the streets that night.

What started the massacre? No one knows for sure. Some say a soldier hit a man. Others say a boy threw the first punch. What we do know is that people were throwing snowballs at a soldier. He called for other soldiers to help him. Soon eight to 10 soldiers faced the crowd. They drew their guns.

What happened next is not clear. The colonists claimed they heard the soldier yell, "Fire!" But the soldiers claimed they heard the firehouse bell ring and someone shout, "Fire!"

What we *do* know is that eight of the King's soldiers and their captain shot into the crowd. Five colonists died. One victim was a 17-year-old boy. The colonists were shocked that the soldiers shot them. No one could believe it!

On that cold night on King Street, the snow ran red with the blood of the dead and wounded.

The newspapers called it, "The Boston Massacre." This attack was the first step in a steady but sure path to war between the colonists and the King.

A New Country

Would you have been one of the thousands of people who went to the funerals of those killed that night? "Why do we need the King?" the colonists asked. "We can make our own laws." They planned to break away from the King.

On September 5, 1774, the colonists met in Philadelphia. They called the meeting, "The First Continental Congress." The colonists wrote to the King and asked him to let them make their own laws. But the King turned them down.

Then on April 19, 1775, at the Battle of Lexington, soldiers shot eight colonists and wounded 10 others. This time, the colonists fought back, wounding one British soldier. That year, the colonists voted to make

George Washington their leader. He formed an army.

On July 4, 1776, the colonists announced that they were free from the King and wanted to rule their own country. The King sent more soldiers to fight for his British colonies. The War of Independence had begun!

Revere's depiction of the Boston Massacre

Attack on Pearl Harbor

DATAFILE

TIMELINE

July 1937
Japan bombs Chinese cities.

September 1939
Nazi Germany attacks Poland.
World War II begins.

December 1941
Japan attacks Pearl Harbor.

Where is Pearl Harbor?

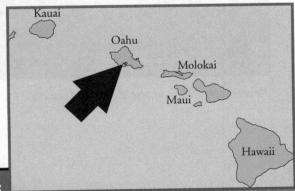

KEY TERMS

allies - countries that join together to fight in a war or for a common cause

fleet - a group of ships acting together or under one control

imports - manufactured goods bought from outside one's own country and shipped in

torpedo - an underwater, self-propelled bomb fired from a submarine

DID YOU KNOW?

Today, Japan is one of America's closest trading allies.

19

Chapter Two:
Attack on Pearl Harbor

For more than 10 years, Japan and the United States did not agree on many things. In the 1930s, Japan took over part of China. This made the U.S. government angry. Our government told the Japanese to leave China, but they did not listen. Even though we did not like this decision, we did not want to fight Japan. Their army was strong. We were not ready for a fight.

Instead of fighting, the United States tried to get the Japanese government to change its mind. Japan had no oil of its own. They needed to import oil. In July 1940, we cut off Japan's oil imports. The Japanese were upset. Without oil, they could not survive.

Many countries were already at war around the world, but not the United States. Soon, we would be!

In 1941, 130 of our ships were docked in Pearl Harbor, Hawaii. The Japanese planned a surprise attack at Pearl Harbor. If the attack was successful, the Japanese could rule the Pacific Ocean. They could once again receive oil. They could then take over China and other countries.

On November 28, 1941, the Japanese quietly sent more than 30 ships 3,850 miles toward Hawaii. This fleet included six aircraft carriers and five midget submarines. The Japanese did not want to send planes from Japan. It would be better to send planes from their ships nearby.

By December 7, the ships took their attack positions 200 miles from Pearl Harbor.

The night before the attack, the five midget submarines silently entered Pearl Harbor. Their plan was to wait underwater until the attack. Once the planes started dropping their bombs, the subs were would fire their torpedoes. They hoped this would help sink even more U.S. ships!

December 7th started as a beautiful Sunday morning. About 130 U.S. ships were in Pearl Harbor. Our planes were parked in large groups. Most sailors and soldiers were sleeping. At 6 A.M., the first Japanese planes took off from their ships.

Just before 7 A.M., some British servicemen saw a large group of planes. "It's our planes returning," they thought, and did not call for help. That was a big mistake!

The more than 350 Japanese planes flew over land at 8 A.M. Hundreds of bombs fell from the sky. Men on the ships and on the land rushed out of their beds. "What is happening?" they cried.

Ten minutes later, a bomb hit the U.S.S. *Arizona.* More than 1,700 men were aboard. Fires broke out on the ship. The U.S.S. *Arizona* sank in nine minutes. More than 1,100 crewmen died.

Other ships were hit too. The U.S.S. *Oklahoma* was hit, rolled over, and sank with 400 men aboard. That day, 21 ships were sunk or damaged.

After a half-hour of heavy attack by plane and submarines, all was quiet. "Was the worst over?" everyone asked.

No! Around 9 A.M., the bombers returned to Pearl Harbor. They destroyed many other ships. Some U.S. planes took off and shot down 12 Japanese planes.

By 10 A.M., the Japanese planes flew away. The attack was over. But before they left, the Japanese bombed U.S. planes still on the ground.

What happened during the attack? Here is the sad news: 21 U.S. ships were sunk or damaged, and 188 U.S. planes were destroyed, never to fly again. Another 159 U.S. planes were damaged, and it would take months to get them flying again. There were 2,403 Americans killed and another 1,178 wounded.

Japan lost 29 planes and three of their midget subs. More than 55 Japanese fighters were killed.

How could this happen? How could such a small country, such as Japan, hurt us so badly?

There was some hope. Many U.S. aircraft carriers were at sea and were not damaged by the attack. The Japanese did not bomb our fuel areas. We still had enough fuel for our planes and ships. They also did little damage to our submarines. The shipyards were not touched. Once the country got over the shock, we built new ships to replace those lost in the attack.

In December 1941, the United States entered World War II.

U.S.S. Arizona

Built in 1914 in New York City, the U.S.S. *Arizona* served America well. Today, the U.S.S. *Arizona* is part of an underwater national park.

Crew: 1,731 (92 officers, 1,639 enlisted)

Cost: $12,993,579

Size: 600' long

Fuel: 10,810 tons fuel oil; 75 tons diesel oil (for boats); 12 tons gasoline (for aircraft)

Maximum Speed:
21 knots
(7 miles per hour)

Armament:
40 guns and anti-aircraft batteries

Aircraft:
Three single engine float monoplanes – Vought OS2U Kingfishers

Japanese Midget Subs

The Japanese Navy used five midget submarines at Pearl Harbor. Three were found after the attack. One was later found in 1960 at the bottom of Pearl Harbor. The two other subs have never been found.

Crew: two men

Size: 78.5' long, 6.1' in diameter

Tower: 93" long, 50" high, 20" wide

Construction:
three sections bolted together, seven rooms inside

Periscope:
10' long

Torpedoes:
Two: 1,000 pounds of explosive

Power: electric engine powered by batteries

Weight: 46 tons

Mother Ship:
Type I Submarine

A Moving Memorial

If you visit Hawaii, you can see the place where the U.S.S. *Arizona* sank. At Pearl Harbor, you can ride a boat to a long building. It is built right over where the U.S.S. *Arizona* sank. There, you can stand over the ship at the bottom of the harbor. It is still there.

Even after 60 years, drops of oil rise to the top of the water. The oil still leaks from the U.S.S. *Arizona's* fuel tanks. Thousands of visitors stand here and think about the loss of life on December 7, 1941.

More than 1,100 men lost their lives when the U.S.S. Arizona *was bombed and sank in Pearl Harbor, December 7, 1941.*

Four Dead at Kent State

DATAFILE

TIMELINE

January 1969
Nixon becomes U.S. president.

May 1970
National Guard soldiers kill four at Kent State

August 1974
President Nixon resigns.

Where is Kent, Ohio?

KEY TERMS

National Guard - in the United States, an organized militia of the states; part of the U.S. Army

draft - the choosing of individuals for compulsory service in the military

campus - the buildings and grounds of a university or college where students live and go to classes

demonstration - a mass meeting or parade often organized to express protest

legacy - something lasting that we learn or receive from someone, especially an elder

DID YOU KNOW?

Today, Vietnam is a peaceful country. It buys many goods from the United States, including planes, computers, and cotton.

Chapter Three:
Four Dead at Kent State

In Vietnam, people from the north were led by Communists. They were at war with other Vietnamese in the south who did not want the Communists in charge. The Vietnam War lasted from 1955–1975. The United States fought on the side of the South Vietnamese.

On May 4, 1970, Ohio National Guard soldiers killed four students and wounded nine others at Kent State University in Ohio. The students were protesting the Vietnam War.

Why did Americans kill Americans? Some of the National Guard soldiers were as young as the students they killed! It was a sad day, and the attack changed our country forever.

Why did the National Guard soldiers shoot? In 1970, the Vietnam War raged. Thousands of Americans died in Vietnam every month. These deaths made Americans angry. In the streets, the courts, the papers, and the schools, people argued about the war. Some felt the United States should let Vietnam solve its own problems. Others felt we had to help South Vietnam because North Vietnam was communist. Some did not want war of any kind.

Students all over the country demonstrated against the war. At that time, you had to be 21 to vote, but you could be drafted into the army at 18. Students wanted to vote to help bring about an end to the war. They were asked to die for their country, but they could not vote.

In April 1970, President Nixon said that U.S. troops would also be sent to

Cambodia, a country next to Vietnam. He thought that the North Vietnamese Army was in Cambodia, too.

Many more Americans poured into the streets in anger. The students marched around their campuses, too.

Things got very heated at Kent State. Students burned buildings and broke windows in town and on the campus during some protests.

The Ohio governor said that the students were worse than the communists. That made the students even madder. The governor banned the demonstrations, but the students got together anyway.

On May 2, 1970, the governor sent in the Ohio National Guard to stop the demonstrations.

Real Bullets

At Kent State University on May 4, 1970, 3,000 students peacefully protested. But things changed suddenly. Some students threw rocks at the National Guard soldiers. The soldiers threw tear gas into the crowd. The wind blew most of the tear gas away.

Next, the soldiers chased the students over a hill and into a parking lot and a field. Then, the soldiers marched back up the hill. The soldiers had powerful M-1 rifles, but no one thought that they had live bullets.

Suddenly, the soldiers turned, aimed, and started firing! At least 28 soldiers fired 61 shots into the crowd. It all lasted 13 seconds.

One former student, Dean Kahler, was shot in the lower back and left paralyzed. Years later, he remembered the tear gas and students running at the sound of gunfire. He also remembered there was no place to hide!

"I just jumped on the ground and covered my head and prayed that I would not get shot. I was shot and then I was praying that I wouldn't get shot again."
— *Dean Kahler*

The dead and wounded lay on the ground, bleeding. Some students helped the wounded. Others screamed in panic. The professors asked students to remain calm and go back to their rooms.

Within hours, students from all over the country heard about the shootings at Kent State University. They shut down their own schools. They did not go to class. They sat down in their professors' offices and would not let the professors enter or leave. They marched on their campuses. They held meetings to talk about the war and the Kent State shootings. It was a national strike!

A Legacy

To this day, no one knows exactly why the soldiers fired. There were several investigations, but many questions remain. Some soldiers said they feared for their lives. But why would they be afraid? The students were not really close to them, and only a few students had thrown rocks.

Eight of the soldiers went on trial, but the charges were thrown out. The men apologized, but the nation was forever changed.

What can we learn from this attack? Some positive changes occurred. In March 1973, the U.S. Congress changed the voting age from 21 to 18. Now students could vote.

The 1973 "War Powers Act" was also made into law. It said that the president could not go to war without the approval of Congress. The U.S. move into Cambodia ended.

The attack at Kent State University changed the American people. Many who had been for the Vietnam War were now against it. Student action on the campus of Kent State University and around the country brought about a major change. It changed our nation's laws and how we viewed our government.

The attack stands for the deep differences that divided our country during the Vietnam War.

A student throws a tear gas canister back at the Ohio National Guard on the campus of Kent State University. The Guard tried to disperse students who had gathered on the campus to protest the Vietnam War.

Troubled Times

The Kent State massacre was not the only time Americans protested the Vietnam War. The nation saw more violence during August 26–29, 1968, at the Democratic National Convention in Chicago.

Thousands of anti-war protesters planned a peaceful, six-day protest. But Chicago Mayor Richard Daley worried there would be trouble. He called in 7,500 U.S. Army troops and 6,000 National Guard soldiers to back up his 12,000 police officers.

As many as 15,000 protesters gathered at Grant Park, near the convention. Many sang songs, read poems, and heard speeches by famous people.

During that week, violence erupted many times. A young man lowered the American flag that flew near the bandstand. Police pushed through the crowd to arrest him. Fights broke out. The police used tear gas on the crowd.

By the end of the convention, 668 were arrested. Dean Johnson, a 17-year-old Native American from South Dakota was shot dead by police. More than 1,000 protesters and 192 officers were injured.

Who was to blame? Did Mayor Daley have too many armed troops in the city? Did a small group of protesters want to start a riot? To this day, the answers are not clear.

Seven men were put on trial. Five were charged with trying to start a riot. All seven were found guilty of contempt of court. Later, a higher court overturned the verdict.

The Siege of Sarajevo

DATAFILE

TIMELINE

June 1991

Fighting begins in Yugoslavia as its states try to break free.

March 1992

The siege of Sarajevo begins.

March 1996

The siege finally ends.

Where is Sarajevo, Bosnia?

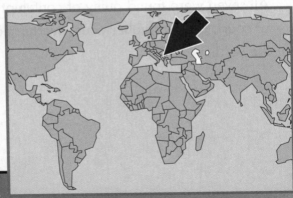

KEY TERMS

siege - a long period of attack

sniper - a gunman who shoots from a hidden position

UN (United Nations) - a place where all the countries of the world get together to solve problems

diplomacy - the conducting of relations between countries

NATO (North Atlantic Treaty Organization) - a group of countries organized for mutual defense and security

DID YOU KNOW?

The 1984 Winter Olympics were held in Sarajevo.

43

Chapter Four:
The Siege of Sarajevo

Yugoslavia was once a peaceful nation in Europe. It was made up of six states. In 1990, each state wanted to be its own country.

War broke out in three states. The worst fighting took place in the state of Bosnia (BOZ-nee-a). Two different kinds of people lived in Bosnia—Serbs and Muslims. The people who lived in the city of Sarajevo (Sa-ra-YAY-vo), Bosnia, were Muslim.

Sarajevo is a 500-year-old city. It was a beautiful place. People from all over the world went to Sarajevo to ski in the winter and hike in the spring and summer. More than 500,000 people used to call Sarajevo home.

In March 1992, the Serbs attacked the Muslims in Sarajevo. The Serbs blocked all the roads in and out of city. Next, they attacked the airport and shut it down. The residents were soon cut off from the rest of the world. They had little food, water, medicine, and electricity. They had no heat.

The Bombs Fall

Soon after the siege started, the bombing began. First, the Serbs bombed the bridges. They had tanks and rifles. The people in the city could not defend themselves. The Serbs even destroyed Red Cross trucks that tried to get into the city. They bombed the hospitals. They bombed soccer games. They even bombed people who stood in line for water! On July 22, 1993, more than 3,500 shells slammed into the city.

On February 5, 1994, bombs killed 68 people and wounded 200, most of whom were just out shopping! The bombing did not stop until every building was destroyed or damaged.

Snipers murdered hundreds of people whenever they tried to go out. People could only go out on snowy or foggy days or at night. At those times, the snipers on the rooftops could not see well enough to shoot.

People Live in Terror

What was it like to live during this four-year attack? Thousands were killed. Parks were turned into cemeteries to bury the dead. Thousands starved. Thousands fled Bosnia, walking 60 miles over the mountains in snow 10 feet deep in freezing weather. They fled to countries around Bosnia, such as Albania and Macedonia.

The World Sends Help

Sometimes the Red Cross and the UN were able to get food, blankets, and medicine into the city. Most times, they could not get in.

The siege was part of a civil war within Yugoslavia. Many countries could not decide how to help. Some wanted to send soldiers into Bosnia to end the fighting. Others thought this might make things worse and lead to a world war.

The UN tried diplomacy to stop the Serbs from killing the Muslims. Nothing worked.

The U.S. government had many doubts about sending in its soldiers to fight. But U.S. planes did drop food and medicine to the people in Sarajevo and those hiding in the mountains around the city.

The Siege Ends

NATO finally got involved in 1994 to help stop the war. The siege ended in March 1996, and NATO sent 60,000 soldiers to Bosnia to keep the peace.

But they were too late to save the 12,000 people who had already died and the 56,000 who were injured.

The siege of Sarajevo lasted 1,475 days—from 1992 to 1996. It was one of the most brutal battles of any war!

Sarajevo Today

After the siege ended, horrible stories came out about what the Serbs had done to the Muslims. The UN captured many Serb leaders. Many were sent to trial. Others escaped.

Today, 300,000 people live in Sarajevo. They again enjoy peace, but it is a nervous peace. It is a sad city.

As late as 2002, there were still 17,000 NATO soldiers in the city to help keep the peace. Stores, schools, and hospitals are open again. Young people enjoy meeting their friends in the streets. Buildings are being rebuilt, but the signs of war still remain.

Attack on the Pentagon

DATAFILE

TIMELINE

September 11, 2001

- Flight 11 crashes into One World Trade Center, New York City.
- Flight 175 smashes into Two World Trade Center, New York City.
- Flight 77 hits the Pentagon, Washington, D.C
- Flight 93 crashes in a field in Pennsylvania.

Where is Washington, D.C.?

KEY TERMS

hijackers - people who take over planes, buses, etc., by force

terrorists - fighters who hurt and kill others using fear to intimate

hijack - to take over by force

air traffic controllers - federal employees who track and control planes so they take off, fly, and land safely

U.S. Department of Defense - the part of the government that is in charge of the Army, Navy, Air Force, and Marines

DID YOU KNOW?

The Pentagon is the world's largest office building. With five sides, each 921.5 feet long, the Pentagon covers 29 acres. It has 17.5 miles of hallways, 131 stairways, 19 escalators, 13 elevators, 7,754 windows, and 42,000 concrete columns.

51

Chapter Five:
Attack on the Pentagon

On the morning of September 11, 2001, Flight 77 took off from Dulles Airport just outside Washington, D.C. It was headed for California.

For a little more than an hour, everything seemed normal as it flew over West Virginia. But suddenly, hijackers took over the plane. They were one of the four groups of terrorists that hijacked four planes that morning.

First, the hijackers cut off any communication with the air traffic controllers. People did not know what was happening, but they knew it was not good.

Some people on Flight 77 used their cell phones to tell their families that hijackers had taken over the plane. What they did not know was that one plane had already hit the World Trade Center in New York City!

Next, the aircraft changed direction. It headed for Washington, D.C., but not the airport! Would it hit the White House? No. As it came near the city, the plane headed for the Pentagon.

The Department of Defense headquarters is called the Pentagon because it is shaped like a pentagon. It has five sides and five interior angles. The Pentagon is easy to spot from up in the air. Like the World Trade Center towers in New York City, the Pentagon was an easy target for the terrorists.

More than 23,000 people work in the Pentagon. They work for the U.S. Department of Defense. The Pentagon's walls are two feet thick, but that did not help. The terrorists used the jet as a flying bomb—it had 20,000 gallons of jet fuel aboard when it hit!

The plane flew very low as it headed toward the Pentagon. People walking outside saw how low it flew. Others in their cars saw the plane coming in too low. At that point, it was only 25 feet off the ground, flying at full speed! It took off the tops of trees and light poles.

At 9:37 A.M., Flight 77 slammed into the Pentagon. It ripped a 100-foot hole in the side of the building, from the ground to the roof—five floors high. Sixty-four passengers and crew and the five terrorists died. More than 180 people in the building died, too.

The people working at the Pentagon felt the building shake. Many said they heard a very loud "boom." The force lifted people from their desks into the air. Parts of the floor broke. Fires started immediately and alarms went off. The roof started to burn and fall.

The lights went out. Thick, black smoke filled the offices and hallways. Pieces of metal and glass flew through the air with great force. Desks and pieces of concrete trapped workers. They could not get up. Some were so scared they could not move. Others tried to escape. They crawled along the floor to stay below the fire. Since heat rises, this was the safest place.

"Within five seconds, the room was completely filled with black smoke. The ceiling panels started falling down on top of us. The floor beneath us buckled up. I looked up and saw fireballs flying through the air."
— *Tracy Webb, civilian employee*

Computers burst into flame. Phones melted into puddles of plastic. Anything made of wood caught on fire. The water sprinklers put out some of the fires, but others were too big and raged for hours. Outside the building, grass started to burn.

People ran out of the building screaming. They ran for their lives! Some bled heavily. Others had bad burns over much of their bodies. "Help! Help!" they cried. Others walked around in shock, too stunned to say anything. Some people tried to put out the fires. Brave workers pulled others out of harm's way.

Firefighters and paramedics soon arrived, but they faced many problems. They searched for trapped people, but the fires raged everywhere. Huge chunks of the building blocked many exits. Despite this, the firefighters and paramedics bravely went into the Pentagon. They sent 70 people to hospitals in the area.

Meanwhile, helicopters flew around the Pentagon and Washington, D.C. F16 fighter jets were also in the air. The helicopters and F16s watched for other planes—they would shoot them down!

By now, everyone knew about the terrorist attack on the World Trade Center. They knew the Pentagon was part of the attack. Would more planes still attack?

September 11, 2001, was a terrible day in our history. The attacks changed our lives forever. The country searches for answers about why the attacks happened, how they happened, and if they could have been stopped.

Flight 77 Hits the Pentagon

Flight 77, a Boeing 757 with a 124-foot wingspan, slammed into the Pentagon on September 11, 2001. It broke through concrete columns and walls that are made of 10 inches of concrete, 8 inches of brick, and 6 inches of stone.

The plane damaged three of the building's five rings: E, D, and C, in two side-by-side sections: Wedge 1 and Wedge 5. The nose of the plane came to rest in an open area between the B and C rings.

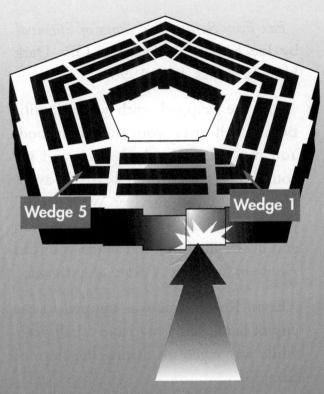

This diagram shows the point of impact where American Airlines Flight 77 crashed into the Pentagon.

Book Review

Fax from Sarajevo: A Story of Survival by Joe Kubert. Milwaukie, OR: Dark Horse Comics, Inc., 1996.

You are trapped with your family. Bombs fall over your neighborhood. You must flee. You look back and see your house as a bomb blasts it away. How would you survive? What would you do? You can find out how one man and his family faced war when you read *Fax from Sarajevo: A Story of Survival*.

Ervin Rustemagic was trapped in the city of Sarajevo for two and a half years while war raged on during the siege of Sarajevo.

Joe Kubert, a famous writer and artist who lived in America, was one of Rustemagic's customers. Rustemagic faxed messages to Kubert to tell him about the war. Kubert created a comic book called *Fax from Sarajevo: A Story of Survival* from these faxes.

Fax from Sarajevo tells the story of Ervin Rustemagic, his wife, Muriel, and their children, Maja and Edvin. Some of the pictures are hard to believe. However, the book also shows Rustemagic's actual faxes. This makes the pictures more believable. The book shows what ordinary people can do when times are tough. It shows how ordinary people have courage. It shows the importance of family and friends to one's survival.

Kubert's book tells an important story. It may be about one family's experience, but it is a story about an entire people's suffering.

Glossary

air traffic controllers: federal employees who track and control planes so they take off, fly, and land safely

allies: countries that join together to fight in a war or for a common cause

Britain: also called England and the United Kingdom; a country in Europe

campus: the buildings and grounds of a university or college where students live and go to classes

colonies: a region politically controlled by a distant country

colonists: people who live in colonies

demonstration: a mass meeting or parade often organized to express protest

diplomacy: the conducting of relations between countries

draft: the choosing of individuals for compulsory service in the military

fleet: a group of ships acting together or under one control

hijack: to take over by force

hijackers: people who take over planes, buses, etc., by force

imports: manufactured goods bought from outside one's own country and shipped in

legacy: something lasting that we learn or receive from someone, especially an elder

National Guard: in the United States, an organized militia of the states; part of the U.S. Army

NATO (North Atlantic Treaty Organization): a group of countries organized for mutual defense and security

Parliament: the place where laws are made in Britain; the national legislature of Great Britain

protest: to speak out against

represent: to stand in for

siege: a long period of attack

sniper: a gunman who shoots from a hidden position

terrorists: fighters who hurt and kill others using fear to intimidate

torpedo: an underwater, self-propelled bomb fired from a submarine

UN (United Nations): a place where all the countries of the world get together to solve problems

U.S. Department of Defense: the part of the government that is in charge of the Army, Navy, Air Force, and Marines

Index